BOUFFANTS & BROKEN HEARTS

COLORING BOOK • 75 DESIGNS INSPIRED BY POP ART AND FASHION

~KENDRA DANDY~

Bouffants & Broken Hearts Coloring Book. Copyright © 2016 by Kendra Dandy. Manufactured in the United States of America. All rights reserved. No part of this book may be reproduced in any form or by any electronic or mechanical means including information storage and retrieval systems without permission in writing from the publisher, except by a reviewer who may quote brief passages in a review. Published by Fons & Porter Books, an imprint of F+W Media, Inc., 10151 Carver Road, Suite 200, Blue Ash, Ohio 45242. (800) 289-0963. First Edition.
www.fwcommunity.com

fw a content + ecommerce company

20 19 18 17 16   5 4 3 2 1

Distributed in Canada by Fraser Direct
100 Armstrong Avenue
Georgetown, ON, Canada L7G 5S4
Tel: (905) 877-4411

Distributed in the U.K. and Europe by F&W MEDIA INTERNATIONAL
Brunel House, Newton Abbot, Devon, TQ12 4PU, England
Tel: (+44) 1626 323200, Fax: (+44) 1626 323319
E-mail: enquiries@fwmedia.com

SRN: R3423
ISBN-13: 978-1-4402-4752-1

Edited by Amelia Johanson
Cover design by Frank Rivera

BOUFFANTS & BROKEN HEARTS

COLORING BOOK • 75 DESIGNS INSPIRED BY POP ART AND FASHION

INTRODUCTION

I have loved drawing ever since I was little. I was the kid with a giant tub of markers and crayons, doodling on myself with gel pens while I was supposed to be paying attention to a teacher. I guess you could call it a life-long addiction! Eventually, I found out that people could make a living illustrating and I knew that's what I wanted to do. I was also inspired by the fashion world, yet didn't create clothes. My two passions came to fruition when I discovered surface design—I could apply my talent for painting in a new and exciting way to a myriad of products. And that's how my fashion brand was born.

Similarly, the following pages in the *Bouffants & Broken Hearts Coloring Book* marry my two great loves: drawing and fashion. The whimsical images you'll find here—mini hot dogs, funky flamingoes, and 60s-inspired bouffants, for example—were so much fun to create, and I hope you'll find them equally fun to color. I invite you to have fun with your color choices so that each finished piece is uniquely yours.

Go get your crayons, colored pencils, markers (or even your gel pens!) ready, and step into the groovy world of Bouffants & Broken Hearts.

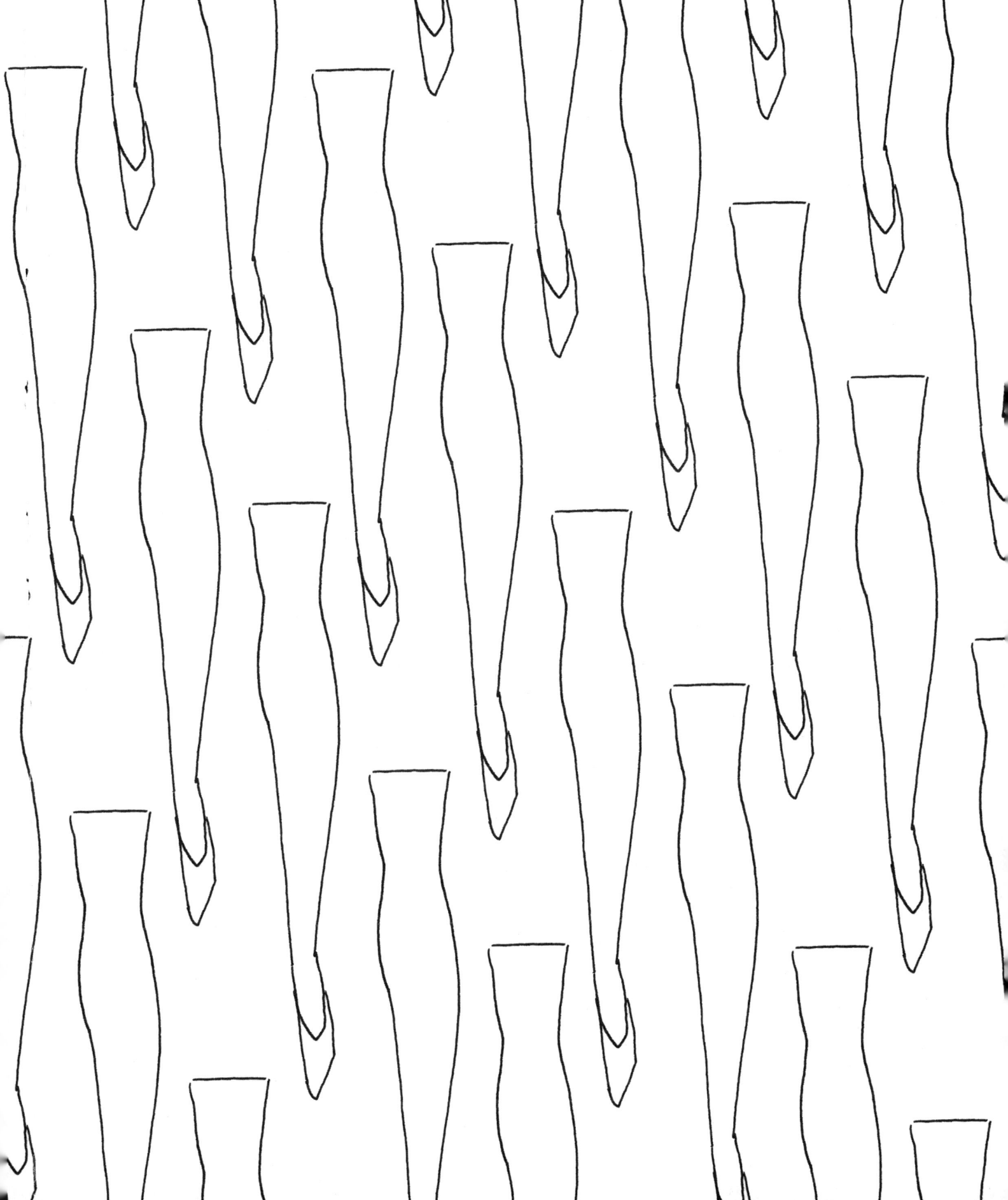

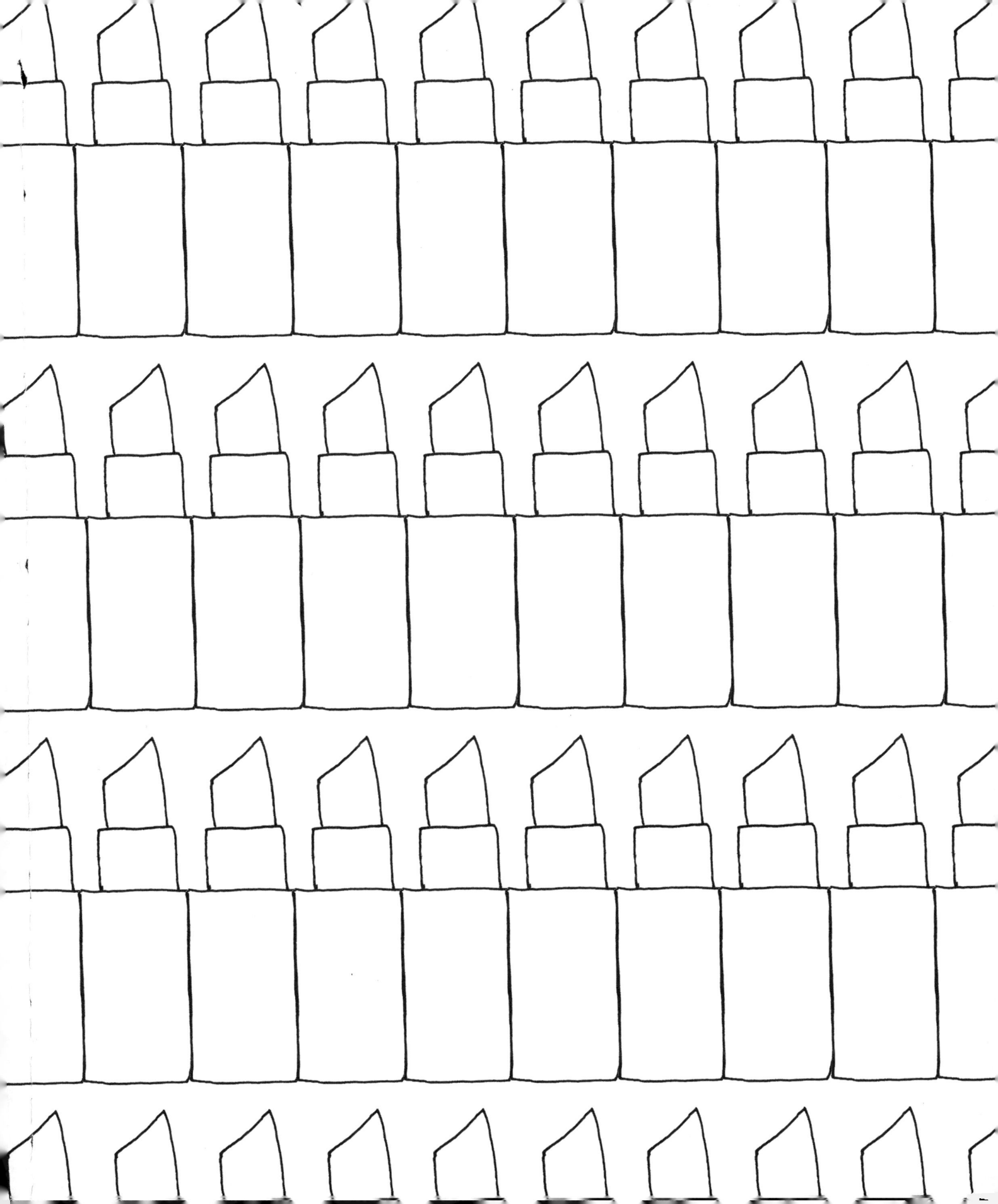

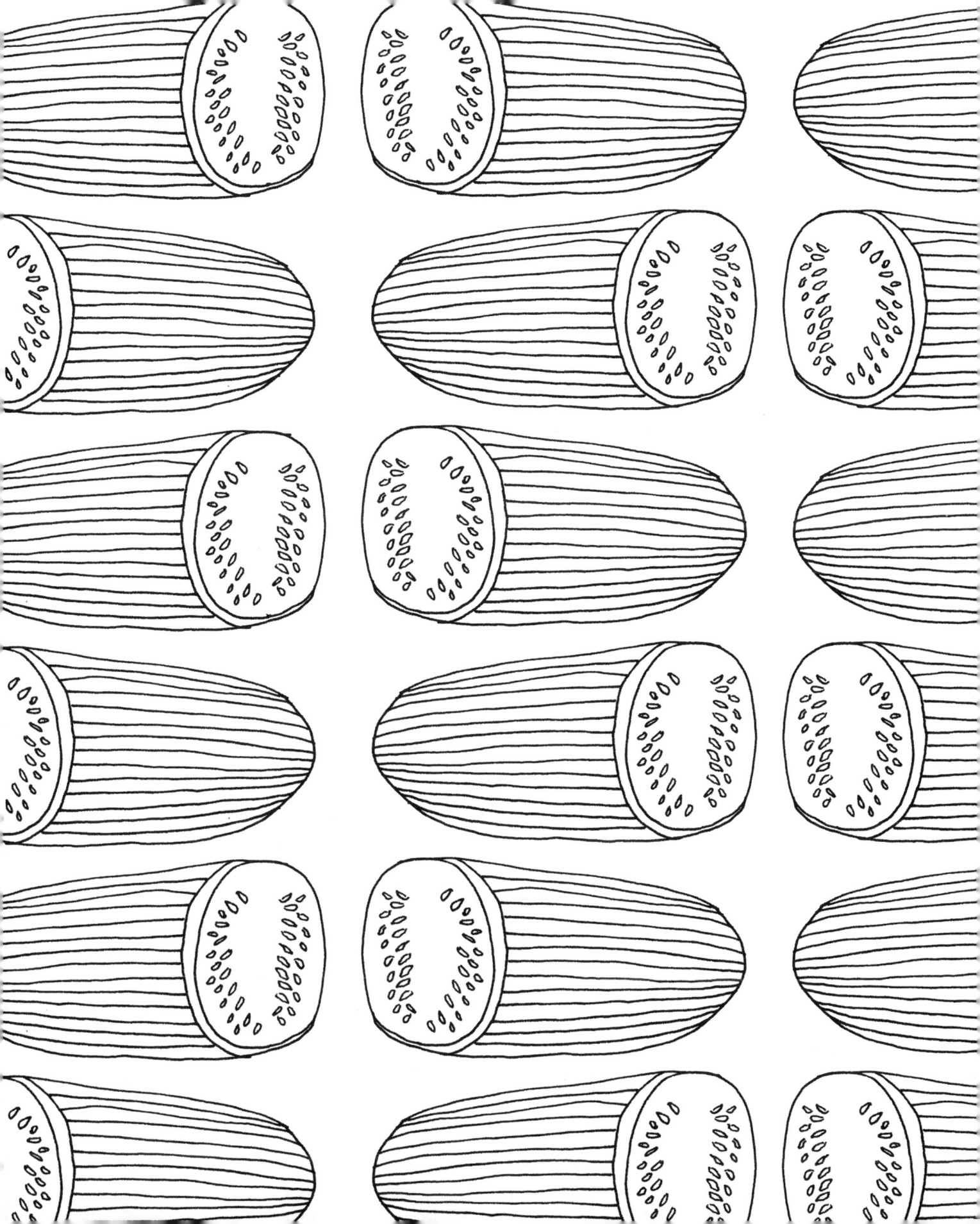

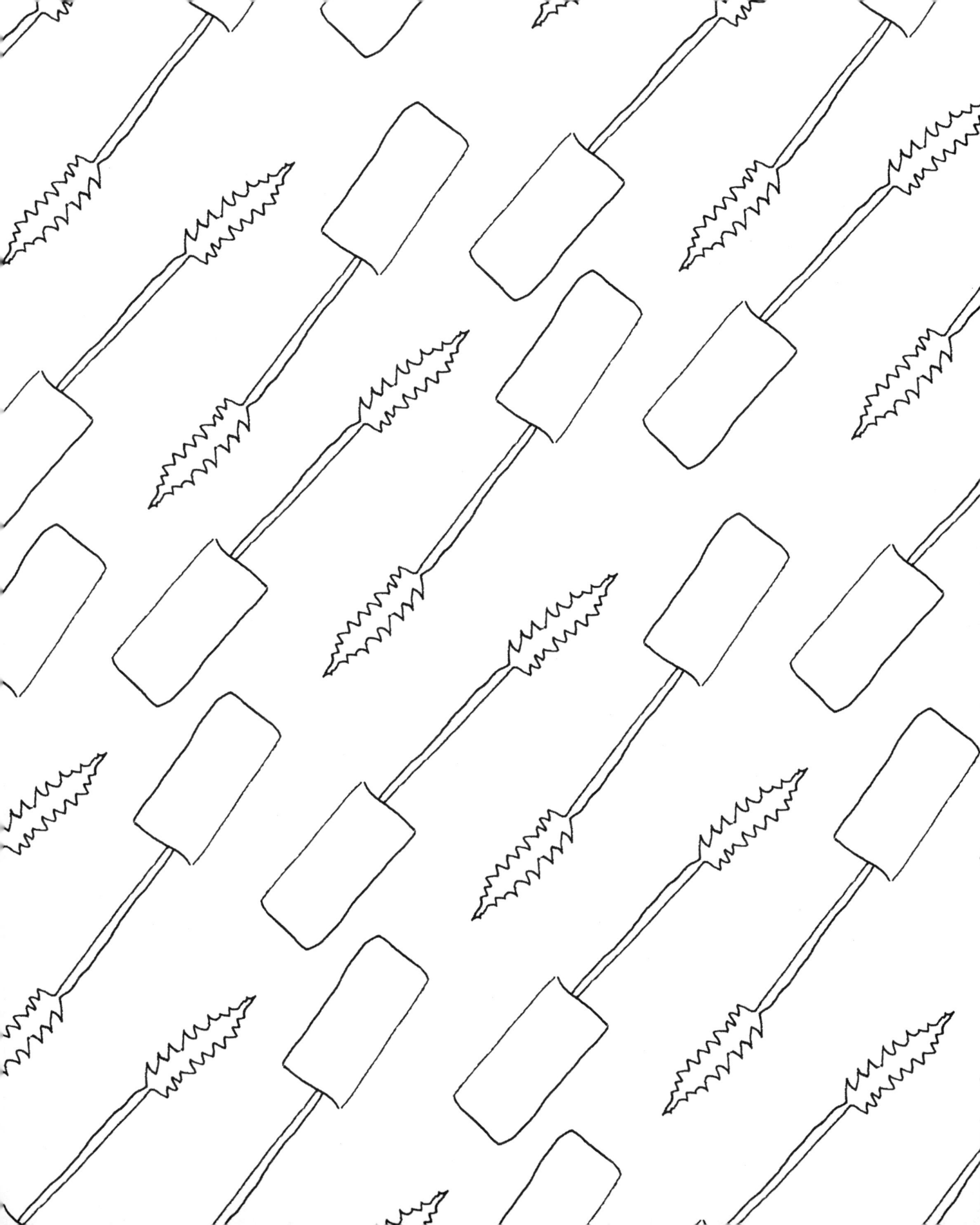

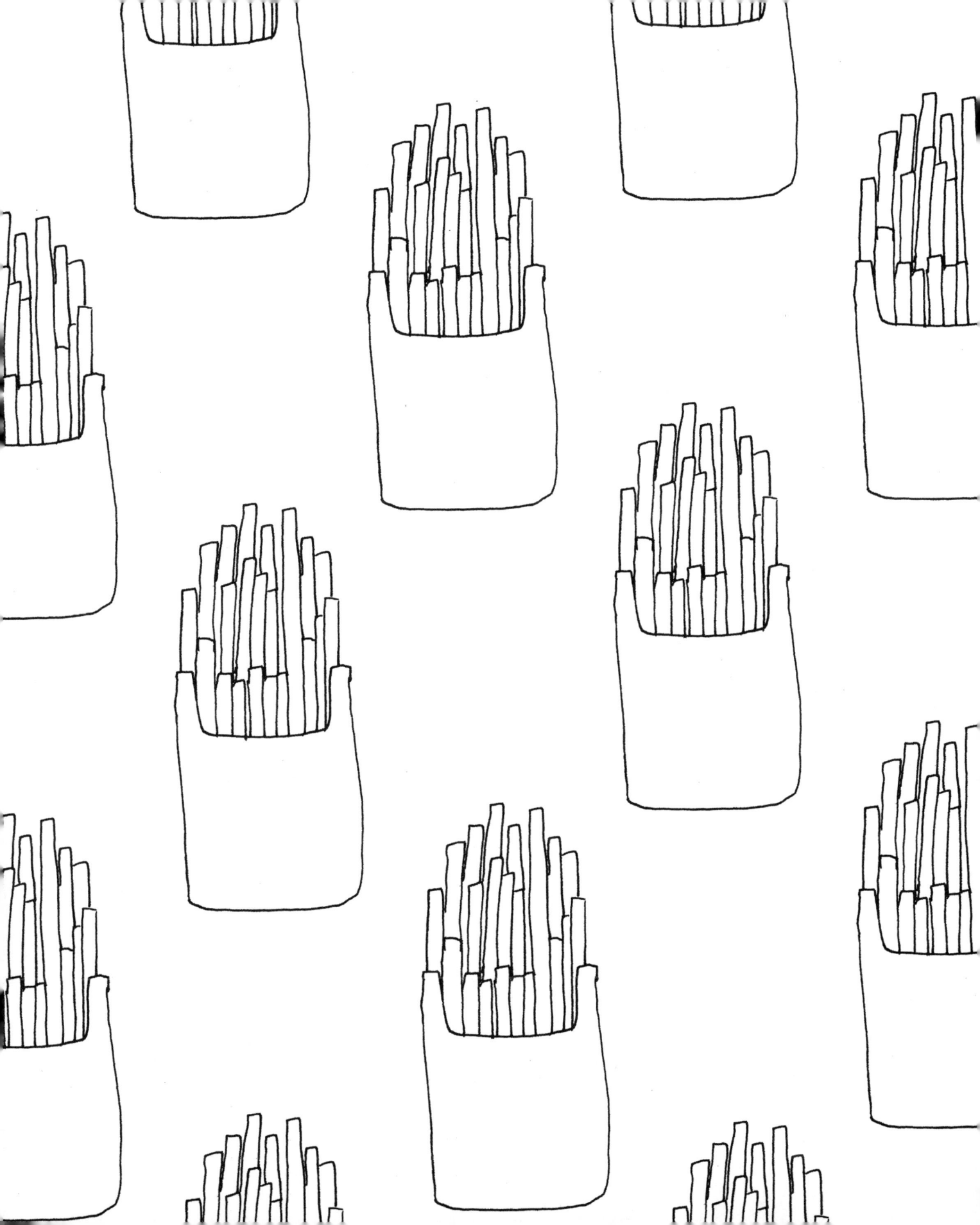

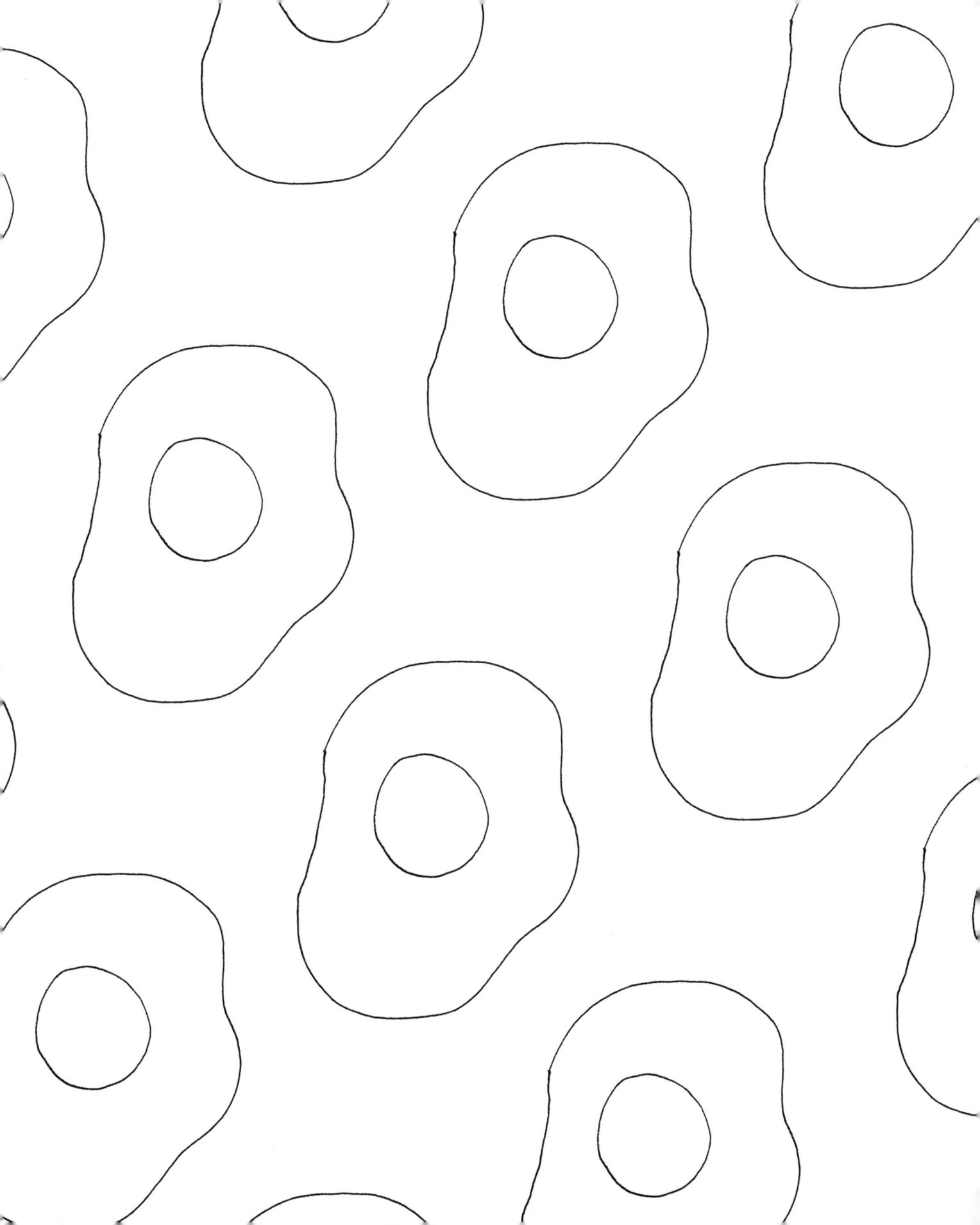

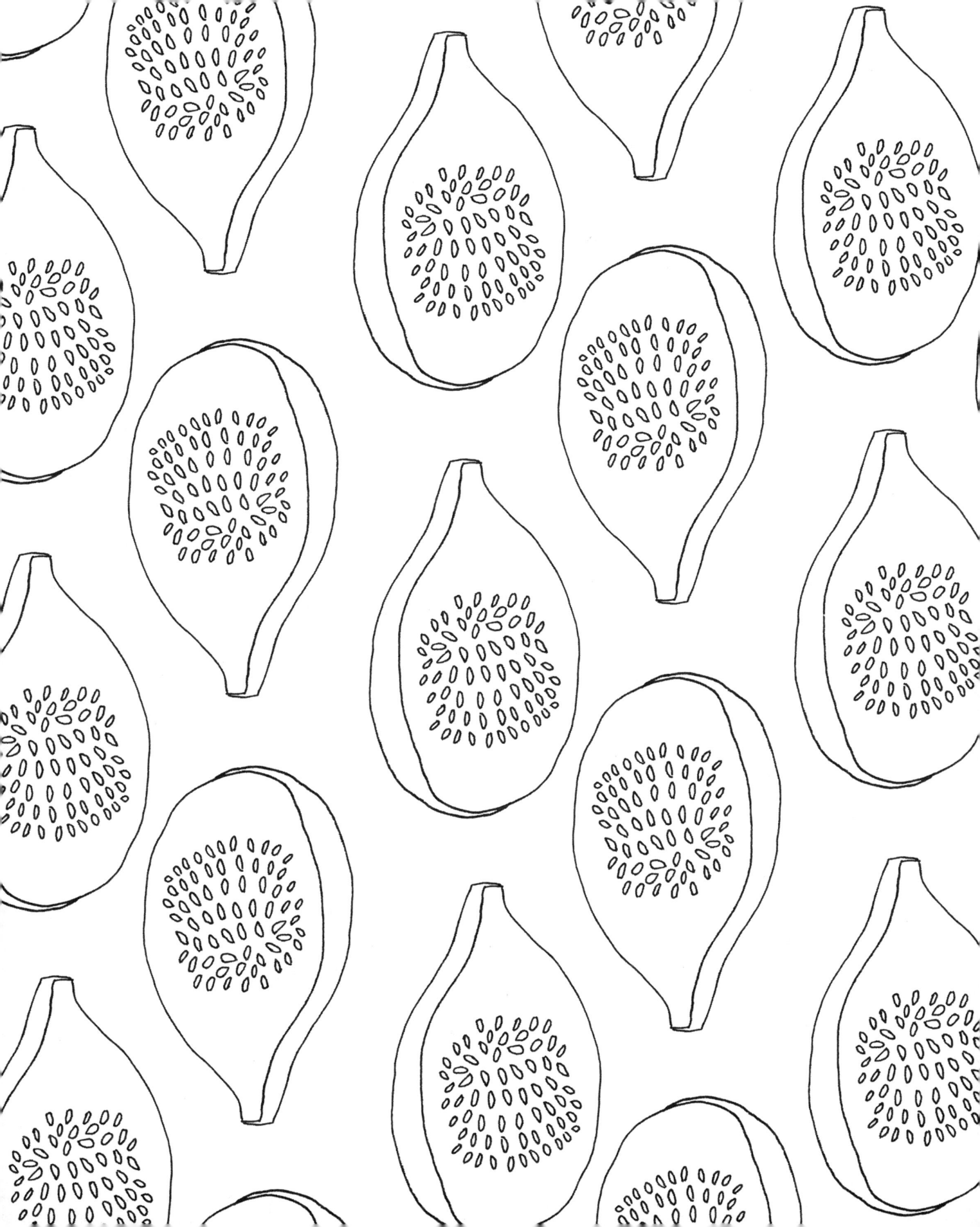

AUTHOR BIO

Kendra Dandy is a surface and pattern illustrator. Born and raised in Philadelphia, she has a bachelor's degree in Studies in Media Arts and Design from Drexel University. While trying to find a way into the fashion world by combining her love for illustration and fashion design, Kendra stumbled upon the world of surface design. This allowed her to apply her painting skills to a myriad of products in a new and exciting way. With an inspired style and voice that is uniquely her own, Kendra created the brand Bouffants and Broken Hearts in 2012.

In a few short years since the brand's inception, Kendra has collaborated with leading companies including Anthropologie, Keds, Nike, Bobbi Brown, teNeues, and others. Her most beloved influences are nature themes such as fruit, flowers, and animals, fashion, makeup, the 50s and 60s, and junk food.

MORE FANCIFUL COLORING FUN

THE TULA PINK COLORING BOOK

75+ Signature Designs in Fanciful Coloring Pages

Tula Pink

9781440245428 | $15.99

COTTON + STEEL COLORING BOOK

75+ Whimsical Designs to Color and Love

Melody Miller, Sarah Watts,
Rashida Coleman-Hale,
Alexia Marcelle Abegg and Kimberly Kight

9781440246302 | $15.99

Available at your favorite retailer, or shopfonsandporter.com.